MORE
HAND SHADOWS

A RELIC OF WATERLOO.

MORE
HAND SHADOWS

TO BE THROWN UPON THE WALL

CONSISTING OF NOVEL AND AMUSING FIGURES
FORMED BY THE HAND

FROM

ORIGINAL DESIGNS

BY

HENRY BURSILL

DOVER PUBLICATIONS, INC.
NEW YORK

Published in Canada by General Publishing Company, Ltd., 30 Lesmill Road, Don Mills, Toronto, Ontario.

Published in the United Kingdom by Constable and Company, Ltd., 10 Orange Street, London WC 2.

This Dover edition, first published in 1971, is an unabridged republication of the work originally published in London in 1860 by Griffith and Farran under the title *Hand Shadows: Second Series.*

International Standard Book Number: 0-486-21384-6
Library of Congress Catalog Card Number: 70-173665

Manufactured in the United States of America
Dover Publications, Inc.
180 Varick Street
New York, N. Y. 10014

PREFACE

ENCOURAGED by the very flattering reception accorded to my first little work of "HAND SHADOWS," which has run through several editions in a few months only, I have been induced to pursue the subject farther; and as many of the public are no doubt so well acquainted with my handywork in the book referred to, as to have got it by this time at their fingers' ends, I venture to introduce to my readers a few more of those friendly spirits or shades, who, without any incantation, are so far obedient, by aid of a few mystic signs only, as always to attend to my summons.

They are an incongruous assemblage; and if Mr. Tortoise felt himself a little elevated to be associated with Grandpapa in the first series, we may expect that Mrs. Gamp will feel herself no less honoured and surprised, to find herself in company with his Grace, the hero of Waterloo, in the present motley group; whilst Mr. Punch will, I fear, think there has been something underhanded, and will doubtless complain that he was not palmed off before, along with his Dog Toby.

In conclusion, I have still reason to hope, that my readers, however unexpected may be the result of their reflections, will still continue to go hand-in-hand with me; for I would not wish to realise the fate of the Dog in the fable; or, whilst laying aside the chisel for awhile in order to cater for the public, incur any very material loss, in grasping at the shadow.

There is one point at all events, upon which we shall be no doubt agreed, that had I been Briarieus, I might have done more.

HENRY BURSILL.

CONTENTS

WELLINGTON.

H. Bursill Del.

2

SHAKSPEARE.

Hy Bursill Delt

3

HARE.

Hₚ Bursill Delₜ

MIKE.

7/s Burvill Delt

MIKE'S PIG.

Hy Burvill Delt.

COCKATOO.

W. Bursill del.

7

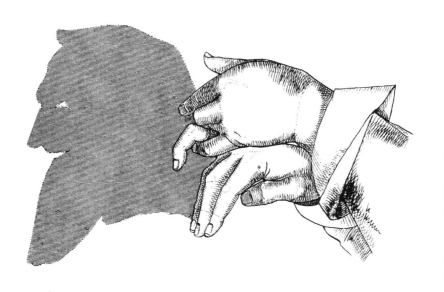

SAGE.

W. Bursill Delt.

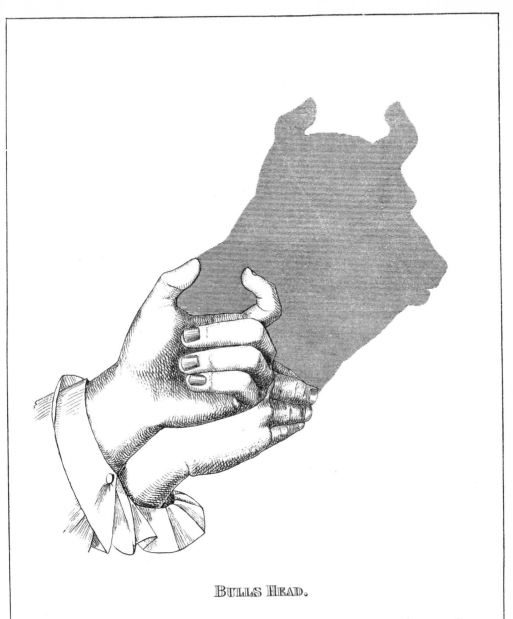

BULLS HEAD.

Mr Burdell Delt.

9

SQUIRREL.

H. Bursill Delt.

EAGLE.

W. Bursell Del.

11

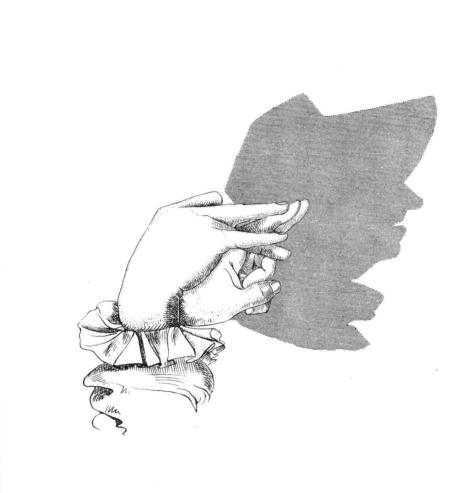

Mᴿˢ Gᴀᴍᴘ.

Wᵐ Burssll Delt

12

SHEEP.

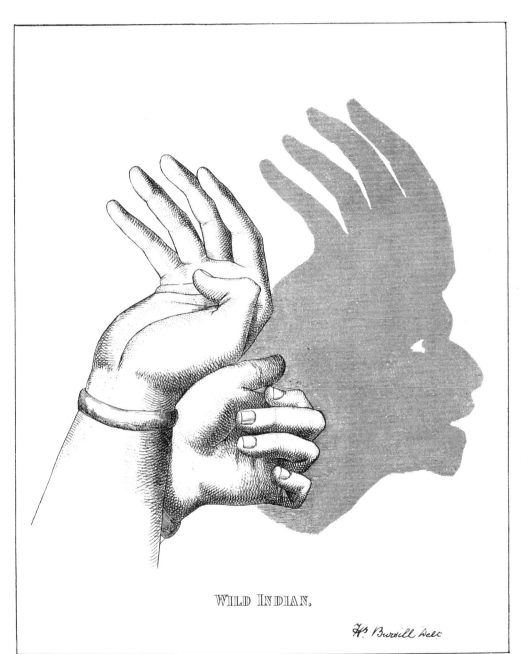

WILD INDIAN.

H.B Bursill delt

14

MR. PUNCH.

H. Barville West

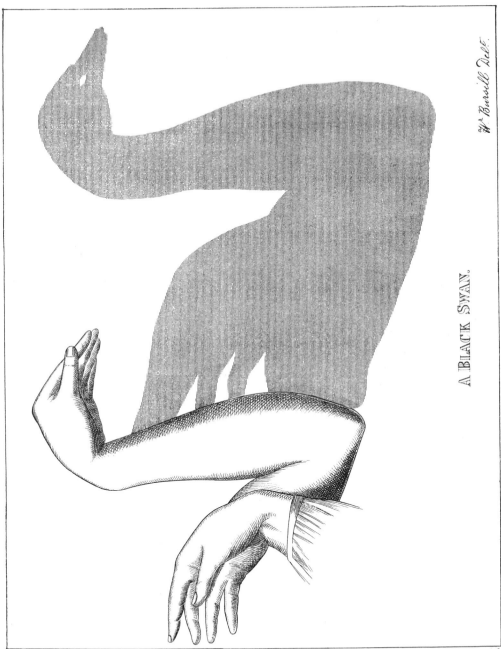

A BLACK SWAN.

Wᵐ Burrill Delt.

16